𝓗𝓗𝓑

PETITIONS FOR IMMORTALITY

SCENES FROM THE LIFE OF JOHN KEATS

Poems by
Robert Cooperman

Higganum Hill Books: Higganum, Connecticut

First Edition
First Printing, May 1, 2004

Higganum Hill Books
P.O. Box 666, Higganum, CT 06441
Ph: (860) 345-4103
Email: rcdebold@mindspring.com

© Copyright 2003 Robert Cooperman
All rights reserved

Edited by Arthur S. Wensinger, Wesleyan University.

Design by Kevin Barlow
Nancy Wynn, Art Direction
In collaboration with the Hartford Art School Civic Design members, Tim Cohen, Erica Cooper, Chad Dorbish, Vaughn Fender, Anna Michelle Oliva, Jillian Portelance, Lisa Roden, Chris Piascik, Keith Vallone and Ed Yetto.

Library of Congress Cataloging-in-Publication Data

Cooperman, Robert.
 Petitions for immortality : scenes from the life of John Keats : poems / by Robert Cooperman.-- 1st ed.
   p. cm.
 ISBN 0-9635185-0-X (alk. paper)
 1. Keats, John, 1795-1821--Poetry. 2. Poets--Poetry. I. Title.
 PS3553.O629P47 2004
 811'.54--dc22
                              2003016277

Independent Publishers Group distributes Higganum Hill Books:
Ph: (800) 888-4741   www.ipgbook.com
Printed in the United States of America.

Dedication

I would like to thank Eleanor Swanson and Herman Asarnow for their tireless
work on and belief in this project.

As always, this book is dedicated to Beth: my darling Ruth amid the alien corn.

ACKNOWLEDGEMENTS

Grateful acknowledgment is made to the following journals in which the poems, sometimes in slightly different form, first appeared:

The Antigonish Review; Bogg; Calliope; Calypso; California Quarterly; Connecticut River Review; Dusty Dog; El Dorado Poetry Review; The Fiddlehead; Fox Cry; Free Lunch; Gulf Stream Magazine; Interim; International Poetry Review; The Listening Eye; The MacGuffin; Misnomer; Negative Capability; No Roses; North Atlantic Review; Number One; Offerings.; Parting Gifts; Piedmont Literary Review; Pitchfork; Poetpourri (now *Comstock Review*); *Poets On; Potomac Review; Potpourri; RE Arts & Letters; Riverrun; Salmon Magazine; Tower ; Voices International; Waterways; Webster Review; West Wind; Widener Review.*

CONTENTS

John Keats Attends His Mother	1
John Clarke, Keats's Schoolmaster at Enfield	2
The Medical Student John Keats	3
Henry Stephens Remembers John Keats	4
John Keats at Margate, 1816	5
Mrs. Emma Cook Isle of Wight, 24 April, 1817	6
Leigh Hunt	7
Mrs. Isabella Jones	8
Wordsworth, December, 1817	9
Marianne Reynolds Writes to Keats	10
Leigh Hunt	11
Keats and His Sick Brother Tom	12
John Keats's First Volume of Poetry	13
The Failure of Keats's First Volume of Poems	14
Hazlitt's Attack on William Gifford	15
Keats Sees the Unsold Copies of *Endymion*	16
George Keats Sets Sail for America	17
Keats's Walking Tour of Scotland	18
Fanny Keats and Her Dying Brother, Tom	19
Keats Lies Awake, Thinking of Miss Jane Cox	20
Fanny Brawne	21
Keats's First Meeting with Fanny Brawne	22
Tom Keats's Death	23
James Rice	24
Coleridge Remembers Meeting Keats	25
Keats Remembers Meeting Coleridge	26
Charles Brown	27
Charles Dilke	28
James Rice, Isle of Wight, June, 1819	30
Leigh Hunt	31
The Fall of Hyperion, 21 September, 1819	32
A Career in Journalism	33
The Fictitious Chancery Suit	34

Keats Dreams of the Inferno's Second Circle	35
Fanny Brawne Receives Notes from John Keats	36
3 February, 1820, Keats's First Hemorrhage	37
Keats's Second Hemorrhage	38
Mrs. Frances Brawne	39
Advised by Physicians To Quit England	40
Richard Abbey Refuses To Lend Keats Money	41
Fanny Brawne Says Goodbye	42
Aboard the *Maria Crowther*, September, 1820	43
Keats Seals a Letter to Mrs. Brawne	44
Quarantined by Typhus	45
With Severn: 7 November, 1820	46
Shelley's Outrage	47
Walking in Rome	48
Keats's Landlady's Cooking	49
Keats Hemorrhages for Eight Days	50
Dr. Clark Removes Keats's Bottle of Laudanum	51
A Sickbed with Books	52
Charles Brown Swears Vengeance	53
Joseph Severn, Rome, 28 January, 1821	54
Richard Abbey After the Poet's death	56
Charles Brown Distributes the Poet's Books	57
George Keats Learns of the Death of John	58
Frances Keats Llanos y Guiterrez	59
Fanny Brawne Remembers John Keats	60
The Reverend Benjamin Bailey, 1849	61
John Reynolds, Dying, Remembers John Keats	62

John Keats, Fourteen, Attends His Mother,
Fanny Keats Rawlings, on Her Deathbed

I read to her in a choirboy voice
so unlike my usual shouting at play,
that at times she looks at me —
when she can open her eyes —
as if at an officious divinity student.
I try to interest her in cards,
but she can barely hold them.

In my mind I stalk William Rawlings
and beat him for smashing Mother's life
like a cracked teacup, for her money.
When she sleeps — rasping as if strangled —
I clench the wings of my chair
to keep from searching out the brute.

No matter that I'm just a boy,
I'd kick him until his skull split
like a caved-in gourd.
It's worth a jig upon the gallows
to gloat at his shattered carcass
just before he's dragged to Hell.

What any good Cockney lad would do
for his poor, shattered Mother.

John Clarke, Keats's Schoolmaster at Enfield, After the Poet's Mother's Death

Barely fourteen, and his nights spent
enticing her with a sip of broth,
a sopped crust, a game of cards,
When her spasms eased, he read to her
in a voice so soft you'd not know
it was the same boy who loved a fight,
even if his rival towered a head taller.

I called him "Bull Roarer,"
for his love of bellowing at games.
After she died, he'd cringe under my desk
when other boys gamboled outdoors.
I never tried to coax him out,
a wolf cub you love
for its fierce, aloof eyes.

I let him sleep on my sofa,
take his meals in my room.
I thought if anything tragic befell me,
he'd howl grief and die:
father, mother, schoolmaster all gone —
and two brothers, a sister to tend,
to break him with a weight of care —
when he should be free
to run in the sun of youth.

The Medical Student John Keats Observes Astley Cooper Operate on a Young Boy, Guy's Hospital

The boy smiled through his fear —
brave as only the innocent can be —
while we students crowded,
the amphitheatre hot as the blood
soon to baptize the scalpel.
I'd set bones before, patients sweating,
fainting when the shards snapped back
after that scorching instant.

Now I stood opposite Dr. Cooper,
who had operated scores of times.
But when that lad smiled
as if at Father Christmas,
tears trickled down the surgeon's cheeks.
I saw, for a moment,
my own small brother Tom
squirming on the table,
and wanted to escape
with him riding my back —
the jockey of our childhood races.

Cooper turned away, wiped his face,
and when he turned back
the eyes of a stooping hawk.
At the first incision,
the power of the possessed
levitated that betrayed torso,
but not a scream from lips clamped
in tooth-shattering trust.

"Blame God," Cooper muttered,
"for making flesh fail,
the need for such an insult as this
to thin, pale tissue,
frail enough without the blade."

Henry Stephens Remembers John Keats
from Their Days at Guy's Hospital

Why he ever attended a lecture
I'll never know: Poetry his shining Lady;
surgery, a serpent he handled
with thick gloves.

His opinion of his place in the pantheon
was huge as the stone dragon sculpting
the boundary of old London.
His verses were no better
than my own green efforts,
but he barely let his eye rest
on the odes I showed him;
he yawned, "Stick to surgery,"
as if saving lives were no better
than stuffing sausages.

He died young, ignored.
I could gloat at my own success
as a saviour among the sick.
Still, when I read the thin volume
his friends conspired to publish,
I'm amazed by the brilliance:

A soaring above his early doggerel,
when he should have been tracing
the course blood makes,
the harbours of inner organs,
whose names flew from his brain
when he was made to rise, face red
as the cross of Spenser's knight,
the rest of us laughing
when the lecturer dismissed him with,

"Take your seat, Mr. Keats,
if you can recall where you left it."

John Keats Lies Awake in His Rented Room at Margate, 1816

The sea — more varied in its monotony
than all my feeble attempts at verse —
laughs at my reams of unmarked foolscap,
the ink drying from disuse in its well,
my quill mourning the fowl
it was plucked from to make a pen
for a dullard like me, useless to myself,
my brothers, sister, the indifferent world
I'd soothe with song, if only
the aloof Muse would whisper *something*.

I clamp myself to the desk,
then give up and tramp the shore
feeling guilty pleasure as I slide
down the silting cliffs to the beach,
hear daughters of tea merchants laugh
as waves rush like fawning hounds;
their mothers stare at me
as if a Cockney murderer.

Does the surf care if one more madman
tacks into the hurricane of Poetry?
Of course not, so why bother? I ask myself.
Just put blinders on, take up the scalpel,
and make something useful of your life.

But rhymes flutter about my head —
butterflies I can never grasp.
I sit on the sand, open my Spenser
and despair, beat my head and try
to toss the volume into the sea,
but an old voice calls, "Join us,
Little Sir John, if you dare!"

Mrs. Emma Cook of Carrisbrooke, Isle of Wight, 24 April 1817

When Mr. Keats leapt up my stairs,
more chamois than man, he stopped
before the painting of Shakespeare
another lodger had left in lieu of rent:
lowering himself with bedding
into a stolen dinghy, various items missing,
girls growing plump as pears months later.

I insisted Mr. Keats pay in advance,
but when he saw that portrait,
I thought he'd fall into heathen worship.
I let him keep it in his room,
heard him ask it advice, weep
when nothing of his own verse came,
until I tired of listening at his door.

Then yesterday, after days of scribbling
notes to his brothers and friends,
of crumpling papers empty
but for a crossed-out word
to waste good packing, he announces,
"It's Shakespeare's birthday; I must leave!"
his hair as if he'd spent a night
in our ruined castle's haunted dungeons.

He begged me for the portrait,
strange, raving boy, in need of a trade
and a sweet wife, like my niece,
but there's plenty of steady local gentlemen
for her to choose from, all in good time.

John Keats Remembers His First Meeting with Leigh Hunt

A paradise to listen to Hunt,
to whom I should bend a vassal's knee
for his prison martyrdom: hounded
by the Prince Regent for censuring
in print that licentious bully.

Hunt laughed away his sentence —
was allowed wife, children,
to paper his cell walls
into a Park Lane drawing room,
kept a library so laden with volumes
the bowed shelves threatened greater harm
than the Prince's brute minions,
entertained the best minds in England.

Then Hunt turned to my pitiful verses,
praised my Chapman sonnet as if Spenser
had laboured years to perfect an epic;
I blushed to confess —
and he gasped astonishment —
to my dashing it off in a footrace
with my feeble memory:

"'Silent, upon a peak in Darien,'"
he breathed. "That is *fine!*"
too courteous in proclaiming
the line a pure, fiery gem.

On my way out, I barked a shin
on a piece of furniture,
and waved away his wife and daughters,
who would have mummified me in bandages
had I not insisted the skin was unbroken.

When I reached my slum lodgings, noise
and filth hit me like kicks from a carthorse.

Mrs. Isabella Jones Remembers John Keats

I refused him with flippancies.
Mr. O'Callaghan would have stormed,
reclaimed my rooms, gowns, volumes, harp.
I shuddered to think of his finding out,
undemanding old man: our summers in Hastings,
the rest of the year mine, and discretion's.

Mr. Keats was all curiosity, whetted
by my refusal to answer his questions,
my reciting whole scenes from Shakespeare,
my eyes darting pleasure at his admiration.

Brilliant, penniless boy,
I dissuaded him with sympathetic chatter
about his ailing brother,
listened to him pour his hopes and fears,
and allowed him to kiss me, once,
the briefest brush of hummingbirds.
My heart thrummed airs of rebellion
the Irish sing in secret conspiracies.

When he tried to claim a second kiss,
I sent him home with a touch
of my fingers upon his palm, some cool words
on our different ages, his pure ambition.
I cursed Mr. O'Callaghan and safety;
my bed, that night, a digging mesh,
floorboards groaned
as I paced back and forth.

Wordsworth Remembers His First Meeting with Keats: London, December, 1817

He chanted – pacing
like an apprentice Druid –
his "Hymn to Pan," from *Endymion*,
a lush assonant gibberish of paganism.
I stuttered some praise to the lad,
terrier-earnest to become a poet,
each utterance from his lips
a petition for immortality.
My first inclination was to cuff him,
so prickly does London make me
during even the Festive Season.

Still, he shows promise; had I only
that first volume to judge by,
the one he sent me in worship,
I'd advise a practical profession.
This heathen ode shows more
than a bulldog-grim desire for fame,
our Age littered with men ravished
by their own swoonings into verse.

Keats, at least, can quote Milton,
Shakespeare, and of course, me.
His couplets not wholly devoid
of spontaneity, but he must drop
his pagan rhapsodizing
and write of plain rural folk.

Later, I recited my "Ballad of Rob Roy,"
a nudge in the right direction.
Let Scott try, in five hundred pages,
to get the times and the man better
than I did in a few perfect lines.

Marianne Reynolds Writes to Keats About Her Ex-Suitor, Benjamin Bailey

Mamma rages and Jane foams;
brother John rants — Laertes-mad
to avenge dead, jilted Ophelia —
to speak of Mr. Bailey:
who courted me with sermons and stares.

Now, if you, John, had reclined
by my side in some green bower
and quoted Shakespeare
or your own dear sonnets, who knows
what tastes might have mingled
in our mouths and hearts.

I jest; in no way inconvenienced
by the news Mamma has not stopped
shouting — more victim than I
of the flighty Reverend Bailey,
who has wed the Bishop
of Carlisle's daughter.

I tell her — yet she will not hear —
I'm relieved he has wooed and won
too far north to be a nuisance
of sweaty forehead and damp lips
mouthing Ecclesiastes.

Had he not sat coiled as a cobra
to strike me with his minister's lust,
I might have laughed
when he talked of chaste romance.

Should you come courting, John —
the growl of famished devotion
echoing in your pale throat —
can you guess what answer I'd give?

Leigh Hunt and the Incident of the Crowns with Keats

Once, after a sonnet competition,
I suggested we exchange laurel crowns —
mock-heroes of poetry.
All serious, he set the wreath on me
as if Pindar were singing
a champion at Olympus.
I chanted some mumbo-jumbo
and placed a laurel on his head,
tenacious to sit among the Immortals.

Then, my servant announced
the Reynolds sisters —
fox-tongued girls,
who, if they didn't spread the silly sight
of Keats and me crowned in greenery,
would laugh all evening,
their eyes pruning shears.
I removed my own,
but bulldog John refused.

Marianne asked if he intended
to wear that tree-tiara
until a starling alit.
Her wit turned his face blacker
than the hand of a singed heretic
who will never recant.

Poor young fool, so eager
to fling himself off promontories
for the glory of nightingales,
he never quite forgave me
for making an ass of himself,
two pretty sisters clasping hands
over mouths when he left,
a beaten donkey.

If he'd smiled once, Marianne
would have stroked his mane
like her favorite pony.

Keats Takes the Devon Coach To Be with His Sick Brother Tom

Though I wrap myself in oilskins
on the coach top, I'm no tortoise
to keep out rain slamming down harder
than galloping, lathered horses.
I've been damnably selfish, thinking only
of meeting Wordsworth, revising *Endymion*,
hearing lines like "madly did I kiss
the wooing arms that held me"
even in my sleep, to wake wet and ashamed;
Tom nursed by George desperate for America,
careers harder to find in England than roc eggs.

Smoke rises from the horses' backs,
Satan flicking his whip at their rumps;
mud flung from their hooves splatters me.
Nights like this, coaches overturn like dinghies,
we impecunious fellows riding on top
squashed like rats by shifting ballast.

Despite this soaking, I feel a power
this Lear-like storm can't dampen:
first, the revisions for *Endymion*;
then a new verse romance, of ill-fated love
in old, conniving Italy;
and Tom, well, though I dread to find him
pale as a winding sheet, his smile
lying there's no need for concern.

I'll tease him that country girls
are mad for his kisses, swooning
to lose their maidenheads in hayricks,
if only he'd leave his soggy mattress,
his spasms rust-red as this road;
rain, Lilliputian arrows,
pricks me to cough in sympathy.

John Keats Presents His First Volume of Poems to His Trustee, Richard Abbey

There, I've declared myself a poet.
I'll forget every remedy and slash
of scalpel instructors stuffed
into my unwilling head like gauze.
If not for Abbey's demands —
as my demon-trustee, the provider
of never enough funds
from Grandmother's estate —
that I continue as a surgeon,
I might have crumbled with uncertainty,
opened a 'pothecary, set bones,
pestled powders to cure gout,
the flux, love's hopeless surges.

This proffered volume's a gift
of which he proudly understood little,
and what he did comprehend
he declared a waste of paper
better used for ledgers or receipts.
He swore I'd starve before I sold
ten copies "of this dreary mist
fit only for nervous women
and dreamers who died poor and mad."

Perhaps I *shall* starve,
but I won't be bullied
by a man who wouldn't know greatness
if Milton slapped him with line
upon line of haloed genius.

The Publisher James Ollier Ponders the Failure of Keats's First Volume of Poems

My brother Charles is ever
the poetic enthusiast, seeking
to kindle literary flames from rotting logs,
a head for business like a Shetland pony
trying to race the great Eclipse.
I should consign him to a back room
with his bats' wings of manuscripts;
he'd harmlessly applaud ecstasies
over the guano that drops on his head.

And the temerity of Keats's brothers!
To accuse us for darling John's volume
languishing unsold, ignored by critics.
My God, I've heard that Wordsworth,
when presented with a gift copy,
fell asleep before he could cut
a tenth of its leaves.
I wrote them such a stinging reply
Keats's swagger-bear brothers
shan't try to swat at us again.

Charles believed diamonds were buried
in such mush-sodden verse.
"Consider his youth!"
my rosy-cheeked brother gushed.
"Consider his incompetence,"
I foamed, trying not to cringe
over the outraged letter I had just read
from a purchaser of Mr. Keats's treacle.
"If this is poetry," his quill
slashed the foolscap like a scalpel,
"my ledgers are *The Iliad*."

When I showed Charles the epistle,
he blushed as if Mother had slapped him.

Keats Reflects on Hazlitt's Attack on William Gifford, Who Reviled the Poet in the *Quarterly Review*

Tom insists on reading
Gifford's review, and others
of a like savaging.
I could kill Gifford
for Tom's sobs, spasms of blood —
his commentary on the assassinations.
I try to hide them, tell him I've used
their rough pages for kindling,
but he staggers from bed to search:
a mastiff bad in the teeth,
but fierce to guard his master's gate.

Oh, but it warmed my heart to read
Hazlitt's letter aloud to Tom,
to hear righteous rage boiling.
We cheered, "There is an innate littleness
and vulgarity in all you do,"
though I regretted our hurrah
when Tom held a handkerchief to his mouth,
his shoulders heaving, a Thames
of sweat surging down his forehead.

I said we'd read no more that day,
and made him drink; two faint
pink smudges stained the rim,
the fatal paint far more hateful
than Gifford's gnawing me for a bone;
all over a poem I laugh at now,
when I don't groan over lines like,
"Whence that completed form of all completeness,"
gibberish too silly to grieve over.

Keats Sees the Unsold Copies of *Endymion*

While they gather dust in Taylor's shop,
women snatch at Byron's *Childe Harold*
as if fighting over the best of a day's catch.
Taylor glances apologies, sighs as if to say,
"Taste has fled before wild sensation."
But he gives change and silently thanks God
to recoup what he flung away on my advance.

A madness rushes into me:
to toss Byron's display to the floor,
a moneychanger defiling the Temple;
but women would swoop like gulls for copies,
battle each other with umbrellas,
to paw through his amours with his sister –
and others – my *Endymion* indeed pallid beside it.

Yet I know what I can do,
though critics club me for a Cockney dilettante,
as if only lords can waste their lives on poetry.
The thought of lashing at boils,
staring into ears waxy as guttered candlesticks
goads me to take a blade to my own wrists,
though there's nobility in saving lives,
or even curing sore throats –
like the mailed fist tightening on mine.

No, Poetry or nothing!
Not Byronic sinkings into self,
but Shakespeare's gallery of rogues
and saints more wildly alive
than the ruffians I encounter on London's streets:
falcons and fantastic spiders
darting off the Bard's quill,
and pray God, from mine as well.

George Keats Sets Sail for America

I fool no one, least of all myself,
in taking this guilty departure:
leaving John to care for dying Tom.
At least he can write his poetry
while sitting by the hectic bedside;
and John did abandon me for months
with our youngest, saddest brother,
always promising to relieve me,
always brain-deep in composition.

I wished to see him throned,
but read only mocking reviews.
Perhaps he wastes his time –
Commerce, Finance, Industry:
the Muses of our hard new Age,
though when he recited,
"When I have fears that I may cease to be
Before my pen has glean'd my teeming brain,"
I wept, and scarcely knew why.

Toward the end of my vigil,
I wished Tom would die quickly.
I stared at his sleeping visage,
white as my knuckles struggling
against holding a pillow over him,
ending his agony and my fury at John:
his writing keeping me from a career,
a life with Georgiana in America.

A brave land for men chafed in England,
slaves to dying brothers,
to trustees dining on our inheritances.
When I told John I had booked passage,
he blanched, rage flickered his eyes;
but he pressed my hand in congratulations.
I pray Tom has winged without pain
to a land farther west
and even more lovely than America.

Keats's Walking Tour of Scotland with His Friend Charles Brown: The Ruins on the Island of Iona

For once, the sun warms my face,
and Brown is not mad for a double-time march
to our next scenic view —
a captain desperate to fill
a breach in a crumbling flank.

I lie, head on a knapsack
while Brown sketches, afraid
the toppled walls will fly away.
All I hear are cropping sheep,
wind a luscious sigh to my ears
lashed by a Scottish June
more icy than Martinmas.

Truly, we've come to a sacred place:
no longer a hard monastic order,
but rest for a traveler
worried by the cough
I've not mentioned to Brown
and risk his terrier mothering;
worried, too, for Tom,
nursed by strangers in London
while I trek these cold hills.

I could sleep all afternoon,
grass my featherbed,
but Brown rouses me
as if plumping up a pillow,
to find an inn or crofter's hut.

"And a wee bit of white bread?"
I joke, oatcakes wearing on me,
as hardtack must have on the men
who grumbled mutiny under Cook.
I exaggerate; but a crisp apple,
peas and a beefsteak, Heaven indeed.

The ghost of St. Columba scolds me:
monks once lashed themselves, fasted,
saw God walk among these holy stones.

Richard Abbey Refuses Fanny Keats Permission To Visit
Her Dying Brother, Tom

I have only Master John's assertions
that the boisterous boy is lying more languid
than the sheets they'll burn at his demise.
Clever lads, trying to burrow into the trust
their grandmother left me to look after;
my investments will harvest a grand profit, in time.

They'll spend it all on horses and whores.
A man of business can put the pounds to work,
not watch them pour away —
ditchwater in drought-cracked ground.

They want Fanny for their spy,
to steal bits of my silver and plate,
claiming they're only subtracting their own.
Little thieves! All's locked and safe.

And now Master John pretends
his own throat tickles with a tubercular feather
while he argues himself apoplectic
that Tom's consumptive as a seamstress.

"What about contagion to your sister?"
I parry, and watch with satisfaction.
as he grabs his hat, nods, and leaves —
mortified with himself for neglecting
to think of Fanny's well being.

Keats Lies Awake, Thinking of Miss Jane Cox

How superior she is to the Reynolds sisters,
none of their literary pretensions,
their flirting eyes melting into mine,
then dropping like a stitch,
none of their terror at the least gap
in a conversation — to them
a bottomless chasm.

I should like to kiss Miss Jane Cox,
wicked of me, not in love with her —
to stare into her leopard-green eyes,
touch her tresses soft as Scotch ferns.
I should like to be ruined by her,
quite spent and heaving,
even while poor Tom coughs and tries
to hide his bloody handkerchiefs
under his mattress.

I've never seen a woman naked;
Byron would snicker; Brown described
the night he left his boyhood in Calcutta,
with a whore odorous as the Orient;
he toyed with her breasts afterwards
for another rupee.

I should like to hold Miss Cox
in that cache of undreamt sweetness,
to seethe and char in her arms,
to have her touch me
where wildness lives, even now,
Tom dying in determined good cheer.

Fanny Brawne's First Meeting with John Keats

They say his brother's dying,
so I paid no heed to his snappishness.
He had other matters to think of
than to admire the bodice of my new dress,
lovely though it may be.
I hate girls who demand praise
for their clothes, for their fingers
running musical mice along a spinet,
their verses weeping for dead kittens.
All of which they'll forget
the instant they've plucked a man
they can twine like daisy stems.

I'll not marry for years,
never a man with his own fortune –
domestic tyrants because some pounds
have stuck to white fingers.
Mr. Keats is more to my fancy;
I liked him for his not liking me:
every dandy in London sniffs
when I enter a room, scenting
a fat hare for his table.

Fools, without an interest
beyond billiards, the hunt, or dancing.
At least Mr. Keats writes,
and though anything
but horror novels make me yawn,
it's sweet to hear rhymes cascade
like sun-jeweled streams –
music played for me alone.

When he proclaimed me too fashionable
by half, I laughed and flounced away,
to let him fume and think.

Keats's First Meeting with Fanny Brawne

She confessed, with a laugh,
to gobbling horror novels like marzipan;
but spoke of Byron with sense,
even if she admired my lord
more than he deserves.

She's a female Beau Brummel:
ribbons matching her blue eyes,
homemade dresses more ornate
than Paris whirligigs of silk.
"Clothes," I chided her,
"should keep us cool in summer,
pad against winter's talons,
and no more thought need
be wasted on them."

She laughed at a precocious boy,
herself barely eighteen.
Her impudence takes my mind off Tom,
who smells Heaven
in every laboured breath.
He'd like her spark and wit.
As for me, she lacks
Miss Cox's face and form
or Mrs. Jones's brushing of one's arm,
her eyeteeth just touching
her lower lip, luscious
as a perfect strawberry.

But when Miss Brawne smiles,
the chandeliers glow brighter,
a look in her eyes that sings,
"You, John Keats,
are the only man in this room."

John Keats, the Morning His Brother Tom Died

He passed in his sleep,
no need to press his eyes shut
as you'd pinch out a candle.
Silence like poisoned air filled
an absence heavy on his bed.
I slumped into a chair beside him,
tears imprisoned by exhaustion.

His face wax-pallid above the blanket,
I kissed his melting jaw:
the exuberant terrier of our boyhoods,
climber of anything with bark and branches,
gobbler of tarts and Mother's kisses,
bulldog-loyal to my pathetic verses.

The door bounced open as I lunged out,
hoar frost on all the railings;
coal-smudged London sky for once pure
as the lanes surrounding Enfield.
I ran, stopped, smashed my head
against a stone façade, punched,
kicked it as if a school bully,
and felt nothing.
A window flew open; I darted away,
not daring a backward glance
until I reached Brown's door.

He dabbed my bloody face, brought coffee,
tea, something – scalding or frigid.
Still, no tears purged me with wet flames.
He wrote the necessary notes,
left for a few hours, and said –
upon his return, my shoulders aching
from having slept in that chair –
"The arrangements have all been made."

Tears shook me like enraged mastiffs,
to hear finality in his consoling voice.

James Rice Dances the Night Away at a Ball

Women giggle that my steps lumber
like a miner drunk with the dark.
Keats says I dance like a deaf man.
Still, I love to battle the music,
turning waltz into polka or reel.
A man who pores over crumbling law books,
whose life is a long failing of health –
has to dance, to forget Brother Death
sits by his bedpost most mornings.
Let me live long enough, I shout,
to be of use to my friends:
Reynolds financially secure to afford a wife;
Keats guided past pike-hungry versifiers.

Trust none in the school of letters, I admonish him:
not Wordsworth, who sees genius only in his own mirror;
nor Hunt, who'd watch his daughters murdered
if the killers praised his latest poem
or pamphlet in an influential review;
nor Shelley, who'd donate his father's fortune
to any charity, but ignores the bills
put to him by honest tradesmen;
and never Byron, who equates betrayals
with arrows of wit.

Oh, John, I'd save you from them all,
but I'm too weak from untangling estates,
from mad dashes across the dance floor.
I can only marvel how great your poetry will be,
and plunge through nights of treading
on lovelies who find my un-nimble soles
a joke played on marriage-age misses.

If only I had the courage to kiss you, John,
but you really do love the ladies so,
and men are imprisoned for what quakes
in me, while I make punful asides with girls,
my eyes never leaving the bold boys
circling the waxed floor, graceful as stags.

Years Later, Coleridge Remembers Meeting Keats on Hampstead Heath

I was walking with Green, my mind more
than usually lucid, leaping from one idea
to another like a chamois on Mount Blanc's
highest snow-slick ridges, while Green
struggled below as best he could.
Suddenly, we came upon a young man Joseph knew;
they spoke, then the lad walked on,
absorbed in his own thoughts.
But he caught us up and asked
for the honour of shaking my hand,
bringing a small smile to my lips.
After a moment he left us,
my caravan of thoughts broken.

"That was Keats," Green said.

"Merciful God!" I cried, "Death has him:
hot and cold, dry and damp mingle in his grip."
Green professed not to feel that fatal tincture.
But, like Wordsworth, he was ever a man
regardless of the anguish of others.

Now, years later, it seems to me
that vicious review of *Endymion*
must already have been at work —
a poison slowly seeking his heart:
a man with only wits to pave his way in the world,
none of Byron's titles, Wordsworth's sinecures,
or the good fortune that drops onto my plate
from decent men who appreciate genius.

What a blow, that malice, to his fragile talent.
He might have been one of our finer sonneteers.
Even now I can see him trudging away,
swallowed by grass and horse chestnuts,
sponging awful blossoms into his handkerchief;
his lungs, bushes of thorns, his poor mind
dwelling only on mildew and decay.

Keats Remembers Meeting Coleridge on Hampstead Heath

In a past life he must've been a cricket
fiddling away the long summer.
Ruined though he is by debt and laudanum,
he seemed a man without a care – unless his voice
should fail him. Pleasant to listen to
(but a fellow likes to get a word in every hour),
his voice most musical, ruminating
on monsters, dreamscapes, the Poetic Soul –
a sea of sentences, no beginning or end,
only waves inexhaustible and delightful,
if one can endure the creeping-from-chapel
pace he and Green waded through.

I was after some stout exercise:
Tom's ghost troubling my quill all morning,
my own money troubles starting to weigh
on my shoulders more heavily than hours
of leaning over a ream of foolscap on my desk
whose pits and smudges draw me away from rhymes,
seeing Tom dying hard as flint – again –
spasms shaking him like a tiny scull
smashed by the fins of whales.

Still, it was grand meeting Coleridge;
a Pantheon once, now a gutted chapel
finches nest in. His mind flickers
in and out of greatness,
landing here and there, like an old bee
sometimes confusing rags for roses.

Charles Brown Reads *Ode to a Nightingale* for the First Time

Keats thumped into the house
after an evening beneath my lime tree;
a nightingale had poured songs
into the sky — a tiny troubadour of inspiration.
He thrust some rook-scratched sheets
between books, to make me itch
until he'd leave the room
and I could sneak a glance.

At last he was gone!
Had I not been sitting,
I might've been giddied to the floor by
". . . the sad heart of Ruth,
when, sick for home,
She stood amid the alien corn."

"John, John!" I wanted to strangle him
for his cavalier treatment of such greatness,
a breakthrough escape from the sonnets,
from the plodding couplets of *Endymion*.

This was genius!
I wept for Keats, hearing
the nightingale's plainsong
but not his own arias.
I read again and again, almost
convincing myself I'd written it —
the way with truly great poetry.

Fortifying my hand with port,
I fair-copied the poem for Keats,
watched it dance like a royal gem
in my hand, cramped with awe and envy.

Charles Dilke Comments on the Engagement Between John Keats and Fanny Brawne

They've sworn me to secrecy,
but her mother knows and weeps –
in silence – hoping for a miracle
of her daughter's loathing,
or that John might follow
his brother to America
and forget Fanny in the arms
of some heroine of the frontier
or a princess of a savage tribe.

He'll be a great poet someday,
but in the meantime,
iambs won't cash bank drafts.
Worse, something dreadful's wrong.
I've asked, but he swears it's mere depression:
unable to compose or find employment
with the raving beasts of Fleet Street
or with Abbey, who nags him
like a fishwife to be practical,
but when Keats pleads for a position,
the old brute turns coy as a coquette.

And this sudden vegetable diet,
nibbling quick as a hare
in the shadow of a farmer's pitchfork;
and his chills and fatigues.
He was trained a surgeon;
he knows, but refuses to tell
his friends, or himself, or Miss Brawne,
who will kill him outright
with her fluttery ministering.

Best they remain cordial, distant,
and John to trust professional hands.
I'd pay for his physicians,
but for my son's pressing education.
God keep Keats from Mrs. Brawne –

she'd dote on him as cousin or nephew —
but capable of taking a hatchet
to his head to protect her chick,
as I'd defend my cub
with the last drop of a father's love.

Keats Rooms with the Ailing James Rice, Isle of Wight, June 1819

A circle has been closed;
I'm back on Wight after three years:
one last attempt at poetry
and to play nursemaid to Rice,
who staggers like a stump-leg ghost
while I wrestle with phrases
slippery as oiled sows.

He will drive me to murder: whimpering
like a wolf trying to snap an arrow
just beyond the reach of its jaws.
Tom's dying still so fresh:
his face pale and waxy as an effigy
crackling on a Guy Fawkes's bonfire,
his coughing – that tossed him
like a doll in a child's tantrum –
finally stilled, while Rice spasms on
to make me stuff fists into ears,
not a word leaping onto my poised quill.

I could press a pillow to his face
in the few minutes he does doze,
but he always wakes so cheerful,
so full of apologies for a cup of tea,
a towel to mop his forehead, soaked
as oak leaves after an autumn storm.
My own cough wakes me in a sweat:
half fever, half fear.

Chilled despite the summer sun,
I've begun to emulate Rice in pacing,
Hands wringing like a grieving mother's mangle.
Muttering verses I vainly grasp at –
mere dispersing hearth smoke –
I tread a deepening ditch in the carpet.

Keats Contemplates His Cooling Toward Leigh Hunt

Brand me a traitorous cur —
for his many scatterbrained kindnesses —
but the man wearies me,
makes me hate Mozart
because only Hunt can hear and hum
the Maestro's most subtle cadenzas,
almost turns me against Shakespeare
since Hunt alone can feel
Cordelia's least sorrow.

I want to wash my ears with alcohol
after his rambling monologues
that rival Coleridge's verbal mazes.
Give me Hazlitt, dour as a Scotsman
but standing back-to-back in a brawl
while Hunt would run and later shriek,
"I fainted to hear of your wounds!"

I'm in a bad way: Hunt's harmless.
It's Tom's death that sours me so.
Unmanly to still feel grief's fangs,
so I show teeth to the smiling world.
George's leaving for America
another talon-rip to my heart.
I'm maddened, too, by this sore throat.

And last, last, hell-scalded last,
my utter freezing over *Hyperion*!
Its stanzas the renderings of dead nags.
Milton, Spenser, Wordsworth, all laugh
at the stable boy's stumbling at boulders
they soared over like falcons
in rarified, magnificent air.

**Keats Gives up on *The Fall of Hyperion*,
21 September 1819**

Not a word makes sense,
lucky to have poured out the Autumn ode's
"Season of mists and mellow fruitfulness"
in a brief fit of inconsequential song
three days ago – when it's an epic
I want and settle for inanities like,
"Then the tall shade, in drooping
lines veiled, spake out."

Perhaps if I blinded myself
and stamped out the measures like Cyclops
crushing grapes into wine,
the lines would soak up some poetry.
But when I write, "Saturn, look up!
and for what, poor lost king,"
I hear Shakespeare titter.

Useless, wretched, apothecary-poetaster,
words have gone to earth for me,
as did Tom and Mother and Father.
I read a fair copy of *Lamia*,
its urbane couplets a relief
from the ponderous blank verse of *Hyperion*.
A miracle the same man flicked off the one,
was buried by the weight of the other.

My poetical dreams are a joke
I played on myself, on George,
on poor Tom, on all my friends
who believed greatness within my grasp.
That beast who savaged *Endymion* was right:
I *could* do less harm as a 'pothecary.

I watch the last gathering swallows,
sparse leaves flutter orange and brown,
wind moans in the stubble fields.

Keats Considers a Career in Journalism

I linger of an evening at the blacksmith's,
so much warmer than my own chill room.
The roar of the forge orders me
to cease being a burden to Brown,
who has lent me pounds and advice
like a cheerful uncle or the great Cicero
guiding a youth of family and fortune.
Time to put Dame Verse behind me,
to stop sniveling after advances
against epics I'll never complete,
to become a reviewer of plays,
of books, of anything.

A hellish prospect, but there's not
just my own mouth to fill,
but George, floundering in America;
and Fanny, to be rescued from Abbey,
our demon-trustee;
and Miss Brawne, all very well
to be engaged to a lively girl,
but she must be fed and kept in dresses,
or love flies out the cold chimney
along with the thin vapors
of a stew made of salt and despair.

Abbey vexes me to return to surgery.
My hand trembles at a scalpel's affront,
but it shudders often, chicken skin
prickling for no reason but dread
of touching the nothing in my pockets.

Still, I feel something of relief —
to be finally finished with poetry;
something of hope to earn a living,
though God knows if Miss Brawne will wait
or if her mother will bar their door,
all courtship, patience, and love over.

Richard Abbey, After Informing Keats About the Fictitious Chancery Suit Brought by the Poet's Aunt

I can play him like a lyre:
if I tell him my financial woes,
he'll offer me his last shilling;
if I sigh and whisper of phantom lawsuits
brought by "Your aunt rapacious as an aphid,"
he'll not ask for a pence of his estate,
while I recoup the losses from ventures
that should've paid as handsomely
as his buxom mother, who lives in my dreams.

Yet I detest him for that carelessness.
He's loaned his friends hundreds;
not one offers to repay the debt.
So why should I, who have, as his trustee,
a greater claim than those poetasters
and blind painters spitting oils
like a spider in rage?

Let him ply the surgeon's trade, or business,
like his brother gone to America;
he should follow George there,
the wilderness will either kill him
or make him tough as bison hide:
needed, if one means to succeed—
no one willing to lend a farthing,
let alone a hand, to a man
all the world can see is drowning.

Keats Dreams of Being in the Second Circle of the Inferno

Wind swirled me in great arcs.
Like a windhover scanning broken ground
for the field mouse frozen below.
I tumbled round and round,
now resting in the crown of an elm,
now swept onward by fresh gusts.

Paolo and Francesca blew past,
forever embracing, mourning their sin.
Another figure floated into view,
a creature of albatross grace
beneath robes a goddess might billow,
a face to make angels chew
their chubby knuckles in lust,
legs dangling, offering a glimpse
of golden ecstasies.

She swam at me, her smile a flame;
then I fell into her arms, a sweetness
undreamt even in the greatest poetry.
We floated and dove like ospreys
mating on the wing, in the wind.
Her robes dissolved as if on fire,
the smell of Hell a scorching magnet.
I clasped her in a final fury. . . .

And woke, sheets tossed,
bedclothes soaked,
a windstorm in my throat,
that creature, those lovers, fled;
dawn a grey splash of mud, another day
of dreary English wind and rain.

I wished for Hell again,
and Fanny, stripped of silk and ribbons:
her hair a smoking disorder,
to make me forsake the joy
of seeing Tom in Heaven:
mourning my dream-sent fall.

Fanny Brawne Receives Notes from John Keats
in the First Days of His Illness

He'll break my heart
with his forced cheerfulness,
his writing me to guard against chills.
Mamma asks after him hourly,
calculating the day that will free her
to find me a rich suitor:
poets all very well,
she'd admit if I insisted,
but verses aren't pounds
if no one reads your volumes.

John refuses to ruin maidens in verse,
so his book languishes, while Byron —
who could swim in his inheritance —
persuades virgins to sink,
and is swept on the tide of fame.

John lies next door,
but the doctor forbids him excitement.
Will we cavort like birds of prey?
I'd only read to him, knit
while the thrush twitters hope
and an early spring from a nearby shrub.
I pass his window on my walks,
so he can have a glimpse of me,
but Mr. Brown conspires with Mamma;
he'd keep John all to himself,
a horrid guard dog that will lick
its master to death
with sulphurous affection.

I sit and think of John, amid Mamma's
crocodile sighs of "Poor Mr. Keats."
One touch of my hand would cure him,
but vultures demand his death,
the cult of one more poet doomed
to greatness in fifty useless years.

On the Night of 3 February 1820, Keats Suffers His First Hemorrhage

"This is death," I point
at dark arterial stains on the sheet;
Brown shudders, clucks beside me.
I keep back from him news of the flux
I swallowed earlier this evening
atop the stage to Hampstead;
nausea swelled with that salty tide
and I nearly fainted;
a fellow passenger glared
as if at one undone
by the laudanum I've been sneaking,
following Coleridge's road to oblivion.

Hot terror trembles my limbs
even as the specialist Brown insisted on
claims he can find nothing organic.
I smile at his prediction of a complete cure,
if I avoid poetry, all excitement —
Miss Brawne, for instance —
convenient for Brown's jealous mothering.
Still, I'll follow every instruction
though all I can think of is Fanny.

I fear to sleep — yet sleep's what I need.
I'm afraid to die with not even a whimper:
envious of Achilles and his hero's doom;
of Chatterton, that marvelous poetic fraud;
of Romeo and his night of bliss,
her hot youth melting into his arms.
If only Fanny would steal into my room,
but I'm too weak to hold her.

On His Way To Visit His Sister, Keats Experiences His Second Hemorrhage

Oh God, not again!
Barely strength to clutch a gate,
faintness noodling my knees,
nausea spurting like a volcano.
Only Hunt still in Town,
I tottered the three
short streets to his lodgings.

His children tore about the rooms
like naked American savages.
Yet, to me, they rampaged in a dream,
silent, ghostly monsters, mouths shouting
but not a sound careened off the walls.

A friend of the Shelleys talked of tenors,
I whispered; even that exertion
pebbled my forehead with sweat;
but some tea sent a weak current
through my veins, legs able to move
as if relearning the art.
"I am quite well," I assured
Mrs. Hunt, Miss Gisborne, and left,
teetering as if into a great storm.

When I collapsed into my chair,
blood again surged despair
darker than its arterial flow.
"Dr. Darling!" I sobbed to the landlady
as if to an angel versed in miracles.
I knew by his helpless pity
that a deadly foe had hold of me,
mercy the last thing in its heart.

Mrs. Francis Brawne Welcomes John Keats
Into Her Home

He clung to the door like a mariner
about to be swept into the typhoon's maw.
What could I do but take him in?
At least now, Fanny will see
a match is utterly impossible:
Italy his only hope.

Let her nurse him day and night,
to see him more lifeless by the hour.
Let her hear him moan and rave —
that lesson will instruct her
of her life as his fiancée, his wife,
until God mercifully frees her.

We got his shivering bone-sack to bed;
Fanny undressed him, shriveled skin
like an old capon, and he not twenty-four.
Still, tears stung my cheeks
to hear the cough that shook him
like hens huddling in a gale.

A mercy on you, John Keats, I thought,
to leave this world tonight;
but I hadn't the hard love
to send him where poets wear laurel
and recite the odes and epics
for which mothers have no patience.

John Keats, Advised by Physicians To Quit England Before the End of Summer, 1820

I could howl death awaits me in Italy,
death to be without Fanny
now that Poetry's denied me
on threat of another hemorrhage.
A devil tells me to kill indiscriminately,
to avenge the death flapping in my lungs.

Not certain yet, if I'll heed the doctors.
Death, they assure me, to measure myself
against an English winter;
but death to give Fanny license
to love another, laugh with another,
when I lie cold as the marble
some meddling fool of a friend
will drop over my bones
to keep me trapped in earth.

My God, I'm only twenty-four,
but Tom never saw twenty
and died cheerful as an otter.
I must learn his patience,
though every nerve in my brain
shouts for me to pummel Bully Death.

My banging heart is frantic
to escape the sinking ship of my life.
Oh Fanny, chafe some warmth
into my freezing limbs.
Soon enough, you'll be free.

Richard Abbey Refuses To Lend Keats Money for Italy

He'll die and escape the obligation;
the raven thinks he's clever as my fox,
believes he can trick me out of the pounds
I've borrowed from his estate.
He'll only fling the money at his friends
then expire like Sybarite Nero.

My business presses me for those pounds:
unlucky investments swamping my sturdy frigate,
creditors with jaws wide as sharks
and just as quick to gobble what a man
has trawled for by honest sweat and vision.

Let Keats walk to Italy;
if the climate does cure, he can borrow
from friends who praise his limp verses
while they pick his pockets clean.
Or let him stay in Hampstead and die cheaply,
Mrs. Brawne only too glad to poison him
and marry her daughter to old money.

He's so little the brisk man of business
his brother George may one day succeed at,
with whom this fencing over loans, gifts,
glimpses at the true extent of their trust
is a game that titillates us both.
I could adopt a lad like George,
but he'd make sense of my double ledgers:
far more creative than anything
in John's mangy doggerel.

The only salvation? To grab,
as George has in loans,
knowing his older brother shivers
in the shadow of a cheap tombstone.

Fanny Brawne Says Goodbye to John Keats, 12 September 1820

He will never return alive
from this desperate trek to Italy.
"A London winter as good as tossing him
into the snow," Dr. Bree declared.
One look at John and I thought,
"Don't leave, love;
I'll care for your last needs
better than any stranger."

It frightened me to see him,
a twitching, naked ash, full
of robust leaves a few months ago.
In his eyes a cringing resignation
to the lash that will not stop
until the authorities burn the bed
he will no longer require.

His fingers cold as damp leaves,
I kissed his pallid cheek:
dank, wet clay already taking hold.
I forced my lips to linger.
"Let it be the last touch of love
he will ever feel," I thought,
jealousy, tears raging in my throat.

When he spun quickly away,
Mamma knew better than to coo —
licentious as a dove —
that my life can start in earnest.
For miracles do abound in Italy,
land of sun and oranges,
of celestial tenors and wine
sparkling with joy and laughter,
of murals of Christ risen,
leading the way for us all.

Miss Agatha Cotterell, Aboard the *Maria Crowther*, Bound for Naples, September, 1820

We've tacked against the wind for weeks,
the Channel loath as an aged husband
to release us from its dank arms;
our trunks slide dangerous as alligators
along the cramped cabin we share.
Strange to say, the invalids – Mr. Keats and I –
weather these gales like Jack Tar,
while Mr. Severn and unbearable Mrs. Pigeon
cling to the rail, a wonder so much bile
can be flung from two empty stomachs.

Had I strength in my consumptive arms,
I'd toss her overboard, to applause.
She tries our Christian, British patience
with her assertions on every subject,
her jokes about graves and bones,
her flirting with Mr. Keats
and grabbing his fiancée's epistles,
her only half-jests that their return
depends upon his bedding her.

Wicked of me, but I prayed
a gust would rip them into the sea,
to make him forget the girl –
more in love with her mirror than with him.
Poor man, he'll be dead by New Year's.
I'd make him happy; our reputations,
given our condition, unassailable.

Aboard the *Maria Crowther*, Bay of Naples, 1820, Keats Seals a Letter to Mrs. Brawne, Mother of His Ex-Fiancée

"God bye Fanny! God bless you."— the postscript

Let Fanny find a rich ox of a fellow:
a gentleman farmer to make her mother happy,
some solicitor or physician with pounds
to toss on his wife's shoes and dresses;
he will answer to me from beyond the Alps
and the grave for Fanny's least grief.

Severn thinks a ruddy glow
will ruby my face in Italy,
good Roman food put meat on my frame.
I wear a smile for his sake.
He will find his hands drenched
in my lungs' blood soon enough.

I wish for the selfishness
to take Fanny hostage until the end.
With her hand on my brow,
in my sweaty, unpleasant palm,
and occasionally a kiss —
foretaste of carnal feasts I've never indulged —
I could face the terror and pain.

I should have known her in health,
when I had hopes for my poetry.
I close my eyes and see her
at our first meeting:
her fan a hummingbird's flutter,
joking she read only novels
filled with horrors, dark heroes,
and swooning, eager maidens.

I teeter to the rail: the Bay,
Vesuvius taunt my feeble tears,
this cough that could snap me in two.

John Keats Aboard the *Maria Crowther*,
Quarantined in the Bay of Naples Because of a Typhus Epidemic in London

It makes me laugh, trapped by typhus
when consumption nibbles at my lungs
like hares overrunning fields of lettuce.
Healthy Severn and Mrs. Pigeon pace the deck:
he a skittish mule, she a bear
irascible with bad teeth.
She raves of commandeering a dinghy,
making a pull for the harbour.
Let the harridan try, her drowning
will improve our fitful slumbers.

Miss Cotterell lies in a deck chair,
barely able to move, yet smiling at the sun,
warm as Caracalla's baths.
I lift her spirits – at least my own –
with stories of Ancient Rome,
when triremes plied the Adriatic,
their holds groaning with wine, oil,
tales of intrigue and immortal amours.

I watch Vesuvius, and wonder
if its cone will steam with molten ash,
an explosion to blot the sun,
God killing me quickly,
the strange mercy for which He is praised.
Meanwhile, I advise Severn to paint.

"How often can I depict
the same view of the bay?" he carps.
"Look at the mountain," I snap,
"in shifting sun and shade;
think of a maiden given to its crater,
see yourself a priest
summoning the hot goddess."

Keats Arrives in the Campagna with Severn:
   7 November 1820

I barely had strength to lift my head
in this rickety *vettura* bouncing us
from Naples over roads breathtakingly wretched
as any in Scotland's Highlands.
Severn filled the coach with wildflowers,
hoping to revive me with their odours.

A sight greeted us in the Campagna
I took for emblem of this land:
a cardinal – crimson from skullcap to slippers –
stood shooting pheasants in the meadow,
two liveried servants fawning
the corpses at his fat feet.
In England, a man would sooner knock you down
than play the hunting dog to a priest.

I sank into the depths of the *vettura*,
the horses – until they smelled their Roman barn –
unable to outstrip Severn wandering fields
for flowers and to quick-sketch volcanoes,
a fallen-down cottage now a pigpen,
a toppled tree forcing us to go around.
I fell asleep to the carriage's jolting.

When I woke Rome flickered like a witch-fire.
I cried out for Fanny from my dream,
to make me demand – for a dislocated moment –
that we find that murderous bird of God
and have him marry us instantly.

Keats Hears of Shelley's Outrage Over the Scurrilous Review of *Endymion* in *The Quarterly*

I'm told he thinks that review
caused my lungs to hemorrhage:
he weeps for a sensitive plant's wilting,
invites me to Pisa, wanting to play
nursemaid to my blood-bibbed albatross.
If critics could kill with a quill's flick,
not a poet would be left alive.

Hiking in weather mad as Lear
lost on the moors, caring for Tom
coughing his young life away —
those made my lungs overflow
like spring floods on the Tiber,
a spring I'll not see again
in this Italy meant as a desperate cure.

It's Shelley he sees crucified:
the same *Quarterly* branded him
Atheist libertine,
a murderer of his first wife,
an unfit father to bastard children —
far worse than a Cockney scribbler.

I laugh now at the poem's mawkish lunacy.
At least there's something immortal
in my "St. Agnes" and the odes:
what days those were, sitting warm
in Hampstead's eternal summer twilight,
listening to nightingales
and trying to rival their songs.

Walking in Rome, Keats Comes Across
Pauline Buonoparte

As I totter on Severn's guiding arm,
we often encounter Pauline Buonoparte;
she casts predator eyes at our third companion,
Lt. Elton, more cannon fodder to consumption,
but a man upon whose face God lavished a masterpiece.

She smiles behind a twirling parasol
even on days of high clouds that fling
the flirtatious accoutrement away —
and Elton without strength to chase the token
and earn a reward men would kill for.

They say she posed for the nude statue by Canova —
a thing of exquisitely awful taste;
yet undeniable vitality leaps from the marble.
How much more alive to encounter her on our walks:

Her silk dresses barely restrain avid breasts,
her black hair that I imagine lashing my face
as she thrashes above me.
My heart gallops, I curse Elton
and my lungs, as short of breath
as an old man running a footrace in Hell.

"For the sake of our sanity,"
I've told Elton, "we must change routes."
Mournfully, he agrees, yet weighs death
against one Homeric foray with this Helen.
If only Fanny had cut such tigress eyes at me.

Keats Revolts Against His Landlady's Cooking

When the boy brought up the mess
lumpy as a milk-cow's ulcerous teat,
I flung dish after foul dish down to the piazza.
The lad cheered; "The Old Cat" leapt
the stairs by threes, her face red
as all the blood I've lost;
she shouted, fingers wild as a witch
casting a spell on a hated rival,
then flew back to her hellish kitchen.

"Oh God," Severn moaned, afraid
she'd return with a cleaver and discarded offal.
"Just wait," I smiled. "Within half an hour,
as I'm an Englishman, we'll have a feast
the Prince Regent would slobber over,
his chin and napkin twin seas of sauces."
I sank back into my chair,
Severn paced, ready to eat his shoes
in quivering penance.

Twenty minutes later, our landlady herself –
the seraphess of gravies and herbs –
set down a first-class fowl
with broccoli and noodles,
all on plates warm as barber towels.
Severn fell to – a dragoon after Waterloo.
I thanked the Signora, nibbled, fell asleep
and dreamt of lying in Fanny's arms
while she teased sweets into my mouth,
kissed me deliciously with each morsel.

Early December, 1820: Keats Hemorrhages for Eight Days

"Damn you, Severn," I whisper,
"for hiding everything sharp."
Better one final bloodletting
than these hemorrhages
that mean to drain me slowly.

Had I the strength,
I'd fling myself from the window,
food for the curs and rats
that haunt the piazza.

"Bring me Fanny," I cough.
"Send me to Tom!"
Tar-dark blood soils the sheets.
Severn, sobbing, dabs, terrified.

"Kill me," I rasp;
he bites his lip and spoons me
weak broth I can't keep down.
"Fanny!" I shriek,
"must you fornicate
with all the world but me?"

Can't eat, can't sleep, can't die:
Tithonus of the Spanish Stairs,
cursing my love, my brother, friends,
Severn: he'll desert me
on this bed soggy with blood –
too much of it still inside me.

Dr. James Clark Removes Keats's Bottle of Laudanum

His case confounds me:
too robust for consumption,
yet blood spurts from him
despite the starvation diet
he howls against
like a chained mastiff
teased by vicious boys.

Damn these bloody Italians
for making his last days so wretched.
His landlady threatens to burn
his rooms after his death,
demanding he pay for the rented piano,
sofa, and other fripperies
she'll consign to the pyre –
like Hindu widows sacrificed
to their husbands' vanity.

"While there's still life,"
I tried to smile
when I removed his laudanum,
not daring to face his eyes
accusing me of slow murder.
"Think of your soul," I pleaded,
but God would not be so hard
to add Hell to such torment.

He wept when I snatched the bottle,
burst into a coughing fit.
I ordered a compress,
checked his pulse –
the sham miracles of medicine.

I emptied the phial outside,
watched the tincture mingle with rain
and prayed I'd not disgraced the spirit
of my profession, which states,
"Above all else, do no harm!"

Keats Has Severn Surround His Sickbed with Books

Stack them all around me, Joseph,
no matter that I've no strength to read.
Recite from Taylor's sermons,
and give me courage to die
without the blessing
of laudanum's oblivion.

Pile them higher,
towers of an angelic Babel.
I close my eyes and imagine beauty
exploding into my brain.
Up, up, until they blot out
the ceiling's overblown
rose mouldings
that make me long
for demure English daisies.

Books, the only immorality!
The odour of bindings
and uncut pages more heady
than the meat pies
Dr. Clark won't allow me.

A sustenance in printed words
I've never found in Cornish pasties –
devoured and gone,
while even now, Shakespeare's salad
mingles on the mind's tongue,
the flavors of eternity.

Charles Brown Swears Vengeance on George Keats, for Taking Money from His Ailing Brother John

I'll smash George like a cockroach
in a Bombay bagnio: selfish brute,
taking funds when he knew his brother needed
food, medicines, the futile trip to Rome,
filthy Italians conspiring with George
to murder John as if in a Jacobean tragedy.

I'll avenge you, Keats,
if I have to dance a gallows reel for it.
I never trusted that smirking thief
squinting like an apprentice demon.
And now, Severn raves about empty purses,
wrings pale fingers in this letter
that reads like a plea from Bedlam's cellar:
I should have accompanied Keats,
and not the well-meaning mouse who'll die
of terror at John's hemorrhages.

If only I'd seen how ill Keats was.
I thought it was love madness
brought on by the Brawne witch,
anxiety over his brother's treachery,
nerves at the setbacks to his poetry
that will yet live if I have to kill
every critic who sneered at his verses.

George, you were so giddy to flee
to America, you barely clasped
your brother's trembling hand goodbye.
May the jungles of Kentucky swallow you,
your millstone crush you like a rat in the grain,
Satan preparing your eternal torment,
John seeing I loved him better than a brother.

Joseph Severn Watches Over the Dying John Keats:
   Rome, 28 January 1821

Hideous, but I will feel only release,
when you finally drift away
like a thin evening mist.
While I draw your face,
sleep, good fellow, dream;
surely there's a Heaven for souls
who've suffered out of all proportion
to the small sins ministers invent.

Asleep, you're with Tom, as I sketch
the tilt of your head, the weight
of your nose that could mimic a hare
when you sniffed shepherd's pies
in a boisterous London pub;
your lashes long as Fanny's;
hair disheveled from Death's siege.

My charcoaled fingers tremble;
Signora Angeletti clatters pans
in a fury of bad cooking below,
prepares to have the room torched.
She'd like to toss me onto the pyre.

I should escape her wrath
for harbouring consumption's contagion
in the house she believes clean
as any in Park Lane.
I can only glance from you
to my smudged fingers,
can only stifle my quiverings
when you hemorrhage
and beg me to kill you —
my body frozen by your agony,
too frightened to let you drink
the bottle of laudanum.

Forgive me, dear friend.
You'd rather have George
or Brown or Fanny Brawne
for a final attendant,
more worthy of your love,
far more competent in caring
for your last, sad, awful needs.

Richard Abbey, Trustee and Guardian of John Keats, After the Poet's Death

He'd be neither hatter nor tea broker,
and surgeon as much beneath his regard
as Gabriel glaring seraphic contempt
upon the fallen angels of Hell.
Those who attempt a living by the quill
must starve by its fragile staff.
I wiped my hands of him, a mad boy
who should have wrestled for his bread
at fairs and market days –
far more healthy than composing verses
no one will read.

That lunatic Byron at least knew
how futile a profession scribbling is,
just words that fill up paper, he said
and paper burns, ink runs.
Hats, tea: you can put your hands to
and feel the mass of them,
smell the profit in the herbs,
rub the rich felt of beaver
between thumb and forefinger.

What matter if I held back what the mercurial youth
thought was owed him by his grand mamma's estate?
He would have tossed the pounds away
to friends too dream-possessed by "Poesy"
"to dirty themselves with honest toil."

I should have been usurer to the wastrel,
believing to the end a fortune was cached
in the reams of paper he wasted
on ink that will crack and blow away
before anyone with more wit than an ass
will torture his eyes with just one glance.

The Summer After Keats's Death, Charles Brown
Distributes the Poet's Books to His Friends

Oh, this is hard, a final admission
he lies mouldering in the soil
they dropped him in before dawn:
the Romans' way with non-Papists
in that sunny, unenlightened swamp.

This distribution his last, sacred wish,
but I'd crawl the Alps before ceding
a rat-gnawed compendium either to Haydon
or to Keats's blackguard brother George:
the one hounding John for a loan,
knowing the boy was penniless
as a Luddite weaver;
George accepting funds while the first
worms of Death were creeping over Keats,
not a thought in the egoist's head
to repay the debt.

It should have been George and Haydon
choking on phlegm, bloody fluxes
defiling their bedclothes.
I want to slam my fist in their faces –
to think what Keats could have penned
had the years and those parasites allowed him.

These books, in each I see his face,
his smudged fingers turning the pages,
his firm hand making notes,
his mind soaring above mine.
"Come Brown," he laughs,
"try, and climb higher, the view
like nothing you've ever seen!"

George Keats, in Kentucky, Learns of the Death of His Brother John

This curt letter from sister Fanny
makes her your executioner.
For an instant, I gripped her throat,
and not black-edged foolscap.
Georgiana laid solacing hands
on my arm hard as the millstone
that has made our fortune on this frontier
where one must be stony to prosper,
men thinking nothing of dining on brothers.

I tell myself I had no idea how ill you were
when I left you to nurse Tom;
in truth, I would have throttled you both
had you tried to stop me from escaping England,
my chances for success there dwindling
like coins in a gambler's sweaty hands.

Our family's cursed: only Fanny and I left,
and she loathes me for not visiting her
when I was last in England, to raise funds.
I tried to explain my frenetic schedule
in a hasty letter before sailing;
her reply, the ice of disinheriting scorn.
So now I'm sisterless, as well as bereft
of the two best brothers a man ever deserted.

I had hoped you would join me here
where brashness begets wealth, fame;
unlettered men think themselves nightingales.
You would have throbbed like Apollo
in this eager wilderness, would have forgotten
England had closed its smug doors
to the genius knocking inside you.

Frances Keats Llanos y Guiterrez Sues Richard Abbey Over the Inheritance He Stole from Her and Her Brothers

I will squeeze you
until not a farthing remains
in your tea-stained toad's claws.
I will see you beggared, coughing
like John; his lungs cheesecloth,
his hopes crushed by your meanness,
refusing to lend him his own money
so he could crawl off to Italy
to die in something like comfort.

You locked me in your house,
your wife a cackling beadle
pawing my deal dresser for stolen scraps.
I can still hear her – dragging
my puppy off to the pound:
"A charity case ain't allowed playthings."

You're a wolf not to be left
with a lamb, let alone children:
John and Tom dying young
so you could live high, smirking
at your cleverness in duping two boys
who believed every lie you hissed.

Unnatural, loathsome, odious brute.
I will laugh as I light my grate
with the first ten-pound note
I'll retrieve from your thieving fingers.
I'll make you watch as the paper crackles
and turns black as your heart –
your hands dancing futile tarantellas
to dart into the fire –
a foretaste of Satan's flames.

In Later Life, Fanny Brawne Remembers John Keats

His friends have called me
a heartless flirt who toyed
with a rose before crumbling it.
It was he who had second thoughts:
Poetry so much more exacting a lover
than a sensible girl.
Still, he liked my practical nature,
that I could put my mind to something,
if only a shawl I was knitting
or a bit of German grammar.

"Lord protect me," he once joked,
"from girls who swoon over poets;
let Byron eat them alive,
as they would no doubt love
and he despicable enough to oblige."

His friends would have preferred
that I killed myself after his death –
Calpurnia bereft of her Caesar.
That I married happily, years later,
they still hold against me,
that my tongue can flick witticisms
against their malice
they use as further proof
that I slashed my claws at him
like a bored leopard.

I would have made him a good wife –
the tether he needed – had he lived
and still wanted to marry me.
He loved the idea of Love,
but a lifetime of bills,
the rampage of small children
who can't fathom that their father's work
requires a silence almost of the grave
would have killed him
surely as consumption did,
and almost as brutally.

From Ceylon, the Reverend Benjamin Bailey Writes to Moncton Milnes, 1849

Sir, I have just read your book on Keats,
and applaud your effort to make him live again.
But one thing troubles me:
you state I died shortly after he.
As you can see, I am every bit as quick as you —
my veins soaring with three cups of tea
and the heat that trances most Englishmen here.
I slash through my days like dragoons at Waterloo.

As further proof, here's my Malay dictionary,
a language of nuance, but like Keats's verses,
too delighting in the flesh,
though none can accuse I've not played
the faithful servant to the ladies in my day.

There was one, Marianne Reynolds,
a tongue brazen as the Bard's Portia,
her lips the meat of cherries and mangoes.
She teased I courted her with sermons.
True, though I did die to devour her.
I had none of John's lightness that hugged
the world for love of everything alive.

Poor lad, perhaps his last hours
were less horrid than you painted them?
Though an unbeliever, surely he rests in Heaven,
writes poems in the clouds of Paradise,
Our Lord smiling at a soul so free
of the censorial frown I've worn
like my minister's stiff collar.

God grant it, I shall see him;
he served the Lord with verses
lovely and intricate as the rugs
Persians labour over, embedding
a single flaw to placate their deity.
I pray Jesus would not begrudge
the perfection of John's odes
when judging his petition for eternity.

John Reynolds, Dying, Remembers John Keats

"Friend of Keats" — carved on Reynolds' headstone

The Isle of Wight's my final way station:
consumption perched on my chest, hissing,
"Move, and pain will rip you like a kestrel."
John came here to write *Endymion*
at the start of his too-short career.
It's a fitting charnel house
for me to brood upon my daughter:
so small, I had hoped Death might miss her.
He overlooks no one.

If only I had possessed John's courage,
and not slunk off from Poetry to Law –
a calling I had as much aptitude for
as a pig for preaching!
I lost myself in labyrinths of Chancery:
unholy spawn of Greed and Procedure.

Just as well I have no strength
to look out my window.
I'd see a dead-wall
like the crypts of Inns of Court,
not the surf John described in letters.
I make my wife read the yellowed pages,
and see him, face rosy as Homer's dawn.

I pray to meet you again, dear friend:
to sit in the Library of Paradise
where you'll compose odes praising
angel and imp with equal delight,
to make the seraphs laugh and rage,
my daughter clap tiny hands for joy.

But what if there's only damp ground,
dreamless sleep? My tombstone must suffice:
to tell men I lived and died,
and was friend to immortal John Keats.

About the Cover

The front cover is a detail from a sketch made by Joseph Severn as he watched over the dying poet at 26 Piazza di Spagna, Rome. There is an inscription at the bottom in Severn's hand, which reads (in partial shorthand):

'28 Janry 3 o'clock mng. Drawn to keep me awake – a deadly sweat was on him all this night.'

Keats passed away on Friday, 23 February 1821, around 11:00 pm. This is the last known portrait of the poet.

The sketch is at the Keats-Shelley House Museum, 26 Piazza di Spagna, Rome. It is used by permission.

Author

Robert Cooperman has taught at Bowling Green State University, the University of Georgia and the University of Baltimore. He lives in Denver, Colorado.

In addition to the many citations in the acknowledgements, his books include:

The Widow's Burden,
In the Colorado Gold Fever Mountains,
In the Household of Percy Bysshe Shelley;

and the chapbooks:

Greatest Hits: 1981-2000,
A Tale of the Grateful Dead,
Caseworker Days,
The Trial of Mary McCormick,
Seeing the Elephant.